High School Graduate

For Chase, with best wishes ~

Alan

Alan Contreras

Notes for a High School Graduate

ISBN-13: 978-1508794097

ISBN-10: 150879409X

This collection was inspired by my friend

Thomas Claasen Meinzen

composer, writer, birder and asset to humanity,
on the occasion of his graduation from
North Eugene High School, Oregon,
though he needs no advice.

May, 2015

Also by Alan Contreras

Education

College and State: Resources and Philosophies
The Mind on Edge: An Introduction to John Jay Chapman's Philosophy
of Higher Education

Essays/Letters/Other Nonfiction

Pursuit of Happiness: An Introduction to the Libertarian Ethos of
C.E.S. Wood
Concerto in Q: Essays, Reviews and Travels 1982-2013
Song After All: The Letters of Reginald Shepherd and Alan Contreras
Afield: Forty Years of Birding the American West

Poetry

Firewand
Night Crossing
Fieldwork (chapbook)

Ornithology

Handbook of Oregon Birds (with Hendrik Herlyn)
Birds of Lane County, Oregon (editor)
Birds of Oregon: a General Reference (with D. B. Marshall and M. G.
Hunter)
Northwest Birds in Winter

Songs

David and Jonathan (lyrics by Byron Herbert Reece)
Song of the Desert (lyrics by C.E.S. Wood)
What a Noble Thing is the Soul (lyrics by Marcus Aurelius)

Notes for a
High School Graduate

Alan Contreras

Contents

Notes for a High School Graduate

Introduction

Welcome to the larger world that comes to you after high school, whether you like it or not. This collection of comments, thoughts, aphorisms and quotations is not intended to cover every possible subject that interests or affects you. Likewise, it makes no attempt to say all that needs to be said on the subjects it does discuss.

Some of the 90 subjects are discussed at some length. Others are simply stated in a sentence or two. There is no special reason for this arrangement, it is simply the way that the discussion of the subjects happened.

Rather than repeat common quotations that appear in all kinds of books of advice, I have tried to be eclectic and use material from a wide variety of sources, some of which (e.g. the letters of Seneca) are very well known and others, such as the writings of Robert Grudin, C.E.S. Wood, Michael Oakeshott or Ned Rorem, are either less well known or are known mainly for work that would not normally come to the attention of a high school senior.

In addition to my own thoughts expressed here, there are 121 quotes from 59 other authors, not counting a few quotations from the Old Testament. The most quoted writers are C.E.S. Wood, Albert Camus, Paul Valéry, Seneca, José Ortega y Gasset, Marcus Aurelius and Bertrand Russell. Make of that what you will.

Essential reading for a thoughtful human as you begin your life as an independent person will vary according to your interests, but I hope that some of the writers I have chosen to feature will attract you for at least a quick sampling. For this reason I have given detailed source information for all of the quotes included. An index of writers is also included.

I have tried to write with some humor, even about serious subjects. Nobody likes to be preached at.

At the end are a few blank pages where you can add your own notes.

Live well. Be glorious.

Alan Contreras
Eugene, Oregon
May, 2015

$\mathcal{A}$cquaintances

Some of the people you know are not your **friends**, they are your acquaintances. The difference is real and is not well appreciated in today's society. Learn it.

There is nothing like adversity to make clear who is a friend and who is an acquaintance. Acquaintances are all very well, but they drift in and out of your life and you can get along without them if you need to.

That doesn't mean that you can or should treat your casual acquaintances as though they have no value. They are entitled to the same courtesy as you'd like from them.

$\mathcal{A}$dvice

Give advice when asked.

Keep in mind that sometimes people simply want you to confirm what they already think or want to do. If you suggest something else, you may get a negative reaction. That's all right.

When you receive advice, accept it with grace whether or not it is valuable to you or even sensible. It is undoubtedly meant with kindness and to be helpful.

It does no harm and perhaps some good to be courteous to the person who offers advice.

"Most letters from a parent contain a parent's lost dreams disguised as good advice."
— Kurt Vonnegut[1]

$\mathcal{A}$lcohol

Whether to drink alcoholic beverages, and under what conditions, is a personal choice. Enjoyment of alcohol in moderation is a long tradition and many people value and honor it. Abstaining from doing so is also a long and valued tradition.

We sometimes joke about drunkenness, but overdoing it causes all kinds of physical, emotional and even legal problems. Oh, it can also kill you.

Learn and respect your own limits. Learn about the disease of alcoholism and how it works.

"You are drunk!"
"Yeah, and you're crazy. But I'll be sober tomorrow and you'll be crazy the rest of your life."
— "It's a Gift"[2]

$\mathcal{A}$mbition

Without ambition, nothing would get done.

Ambition is good when it is directed at achieving good things. Like many human attributes, it can become entwined with **ego**, **lust,** greed and other things that are likely to lead to harming others, harming yourself or a life that becomes unbalanced.

Focus your ambition on the worthwhile.

$\mathcal{A}$ncestors

There is much of value to be gained from the experience of our ancestors and others who came before us. However, the world that they lived in and experienced is not our world. It has some things in common with ours and some differences.

Sift the advice and knowledge of those who came before for the wisdom that applies to the world you actually live in. Don't try to force the actual world of today into a corset designed for a different body.

"We warm ourselves by fires we did not build and drink from wells we did not dig."
— Deuteronomy 6:11

"The teachings of our forefathers are intended to be landmarks, not campsites."
— Jane Palen Rushmore[3]

11

Apologies

Apologizing is never enjoyable. It isn't fun. It is easy to dodge or avoid.

Do it anyway. You are not always right.

You never need to apologize for being truthful, but sometimes you need to apologize for being hurtful.

Sometimes you will say things when you are overheated that you soon realize should not have been said.

If you say something inappropriate to someone in a public gathering, apologize right away – yeah, in front of all those people. It can be pretty emotional, but it is the right thing to do.

Sometimes you'll say something to a loved one that you later want to undo. You can't undo it, but you can recognize it for what it was and apologize for it.

Apologizing is quite rare these days, in which stomping people's thoughts and life choices in public is considered good entertainment. Do you want to stand out from the crowd? Apologizing is a positive way to do so.

$\mathcal{A}$utonomy

Autonomy means that we are able to do what we want to do, not what someone else wants us to do.

What does that really mean? We are all part of social communities of one kind or another, even if we are temporarily disconnected from such communities. We are not able to exist on a permanent basis away from all other humans unless we devote extraordinary resources to doing so.

In practice, autonomy means being free to pursue your own choices while still being able to eat and have shelter over your head. Very few people, mainly the wealthy and the extremely poor, have significant levels of autonomy. For the rest of us, the question is how to achieve an acceptable level of autonomy in daily life.

In American society, autonomy is largely a function of financial security, as we live in a society that does not value people as such. The more **money** you have that is not required for basic existence, the more autonomous you are in the U.S. For this reason, the lower your daily costs are – food, shelter and related items – the more autonomy you gain per dollar set aside.

This is a crudely economic analysis, but we live in a crudely economic society.

$\mathcal{B}$attles

Fight important battles on turf of your own choosing. The disadvantage of fighting any devil in its own hell is that it knows the terrain.

Some battles are necessary. Some are not. Learning to distinguish which ones are necessary is a useful, even critical skill.

If you fight every possible battle that you might, without differentiating them as to which are worthwhile, you will waste a lot of time and energy on trivia.

Likewise, if you refuse to fight a battle that is necessary to your well-being or your sense of moral propriety, you may wish that you had been stronger.

$\mathcal{B}$*eauty*

Appreciation of beauty is not a felony.   It is out of fashion just now, but don't let that limit you.

Never be afraid to make the world more beautiful. There are plenty of people trying to make it more ugly.

You will sometimes encounter someone who does not meet traditional ideas of beauty because of physical damage or some other factor. It is undoubtedly difficult to live as such a person must. Knowing such a person is a test of **honesty** and **kindness**.

Beelzebub

Yeah, him. Her. It. You know, the forky tail, the cloven hoofs. Big Red.

The Devil is one of our oldest and most useful myths. You don't have to be religious to recognize that there is, from time to time, a voice in your ear that encourages you to do things that are bad.

It's Old Scratch. Satan. Most of us have at least a small part that is willing to hear what that Voice has to say. The ultimate Dealer, does he/she/it have a deal for you (sucker).

Maybe you are not yet on speaking terms with His Most Charred. You will be. Not by your choice, of course. You're not that kind of a person. That's ok, he'll wait.

The day will come when you'll hear the Voice. Be prepared and recognize that overheated hiss when you hear it. It will sound really good. Forewarned, you know that it isn't.

ℬorders

All borders have at least two sides.

Sometimes you will find yourself on the opposite side of an issue from where you expected yourself to be. That is ok. Life is always more complex than we think it is.

If we don't change our minds when faced with new knowledge, then we are not really using **reason**. Flip-flopping? It's called **thinking**.

"We are always trying to become something different, striving for a new mode of being, and indeed cannot remain in one state for long. ... a person should be regarded as a process, not an unchangeable entity."
— Karen Armstrong[4]

"You are going to differ from yourself as differs from a slack rope that selfsame rope when taut."
— Paul Valery[5]

Character

Your character is who *you* really are, not who someone else is or who someone else thinks you are or should be. It is not the same as your **reputation**.

When you become aware of ways in which you disappoint yourself, you will also see ways to become a better you according to your own standards.

Be the person you always looked up to.

♪

"Your duty is to stand straight – not be held straight."
— Marcus Aurelius[6]

Cities

Everything is magnified in cities. Cities concentrate the essence of humanity. The heights of collective culture and the depths of human misery are most obvious in cities.

That's why many people leave cities to live in suburbs—such people are close enough to dash into the city for the high end of culture, but they don't have to live there and be soiled by urban problems.

What are urban problems? Cities tend to attract people who cannot survive in small towns or the countryside because no one will feed them or give them shelter. Food and shelter can generally be scrounged up one way or another in cities.

Also, it is easier to live by crime in cities because more potential victims are gathered in one place.

Yet cities are also the source of a certain vibrancy and excitement and serve to potentially concentrate people with similar interests in a way that lets them interact and create improved futures for society.

"Unsettling business for an artist, where everything that happens in New York has universality, and everything that happens outside is ethnography."
— Kurt Vonnegut[7]

♪

"Think about suburban life. Out in the gated community, one rarely has to face the hard realities of the city. The suburban existence is an exit plan. This mode of living puts people out of the fray."

— Eric Wilson[8]

College

College should not be about measuring what people know. That's called testing.

College is about helping you learn to think, not making you happy. Sometimes this means making you uncomfortable. Deal with it. Life isn't set up to give you constant comfort and you might as well get used to it.

College involves human interaction at many levels, including learning to change one's mind based on new information (critical **thinking**) and learning ways of interaction with others.

American universities today have largely been forced into the role of job training. This has happened because so many people want it to, but that does not mean that the result is good.

A lot of the people you meet in college are not there for the same reasons you are. Follow your own inner light to get what you need out of the college experience.

Unless you work for yourself in some fashion using your innate skills and your *education*, you'll need to use your *training* to please someone else so they hire you and pay you. Otherwise you don't get to eat.

What's the difference between **education** and training? Education helps you do what you want to do. Training helps you do what someone else wants you to do. Sure, that's oversimplified, but keep it in mind.

Our education system beyond high school is mainly a training system, except for some nonpublic colleges and special segments in public universities.

If you actually want an education, you need to track it down in the underbrush and catch it.

♪

"Universities are not fallout shelters. Brutalities cry for attention. Attention to the appalling causes disturbance. Deal with it. You're at school to be disturbed. Universities are very much in the business of trying to get you to rethink why you believe what you believe and whether you have grounds for believing it. ... What ever happened to, "Ye shall know the truth, and the truth shall make ye free"? Not comfortable — free."

— Todd Gitlin[9]

♪

"Most people do not go to college for an education. ... I was going back for an education. ... This is almost impossible to explain to a university."

— Robert Duncan [10]

♪

"...some of our most sacred institutions have become happiness schools. ... While the liberal arts education was once a studious course emphasizing the intrinsic value of education, it is now mostly a precursor for trade."

— Eric Wilson[11]

♪

"My undergraduates' career plans are a peculiar mixture of naked ambition and hair-shirt altruism. If they pursue investment banking, they do so not merely to make money. Rather, they want to use their eventual wealth to distribute solar light bulbs to every residence of a developing nation. ... They dream of engineering an app that will make tequila flow out of thin air into your outstretched shot glass. My students, I suspect, are receiving their professional advice from a council of emojis."

— Jacques Berlinerblau[12]

Compassion

Human misery is visible to us every day. It is visible near at hand and far away. From time to time you may have an opportunity to help reduce misery. Take it.

Sometimes our compassion exceeds our capacity. We cannot solve every problem. We cannot help every person.

It is possible to drown in a sea of other people's misery. Do not think that you can solve all of their problems, or even most of them. You can't.

To be effective in making our corner of the world a better place, we must focus on what we *can* do.

Unless you are called to sacrifice your own life on the pyre of other people's problems, recognize your limits and do what you can, not what you can't.

Competition

The economy and many educational and social norms in our society are based on the idea of competition, that is, that competition is always inherently good and allows **excellence** to be determined and quality to float to the top, where it rightly belongs.

There are elements of truth to this idea. However, it is over-applied and should not be taken as a proper method for all purposes.

"Can a university, or a nation, afford this exclusive rule of competition, this purely economic economy? The great fault of this approach to things is that it is so drastically reductive; it does not permit us to live and work as human beings, as the best of our inheritance defines us. Rats and roaches live by competition under the laws of supply and demand; it is the privilege of human beings to live under the laws of justice and mercy."
— Wendell Berry[13]

Creativity

Many people are creative, but not many have the **perseverance** to follow their creative talents as far as they can be taken. It is easy to write with reasonable clarity. Learning the basics of music or other fine arts is within many people's capacity. Taking those skills further than basic knowledge requires **focus** and **work**. It is easy to get distracted by daily noise until your creative energy is dissipated with nothing to show for it.

"If the arts could express each other, we'd only need one art."
— Ned Rorem[14]

"Creation is the process of moving an object or situation from the invisible realm of thoughts and ideas to the visible realm of our physical world."
— John Contreras[15]

"All serious innovation is only rendered possible by some accident enabling unpopular persons to survive."
— Bertrand Russell[16]

Culture

Culture is real. Cultures differ and are affected by all kinds of factors. It is always difficult to combine or blend groups of people whose cultural backgrounds and norms are very different. It always takes thought and energy and should never be done casually or in the expectation that it will be easy.

Culture is not the same as race and should not be conflated with race. Likewise it is not the same as religion. For this reason there are usually complex overlaps among these categories of humanity. One cannot be used to predict or describe another.

If you go to college you will often hear the term "multiculturalism" used as though it has an obvious, indisputable meaning. It doesn't. Be careful to understand exactly what it means in a given context.

Most people barely understand their own culture and are only capable of a casual skimming of other cultures. Learn your own culture – or cultures – before getting too multi.

Discrimination

Discrimination is not always bad. The word needs to be rehabilitated and put to useful tasks.

Discrimination is a good thing when it means applying your own informed **taste** or **judgment** to a given work of art, offering of food, piece of music or in any other situation in which qualitative **evaluation** can be exercised based on an acceptable **standard**.

Your idea of what constitutes an acceptable standard will differ from that of other people. Some people will tell you that the mere idea that there is such a thing as a standard is wrong, and to try to apply your judgment and discrimination using such a standard is wrong. These ideas are common in schools and universities. They are incorrect.

What is bad is *irrational* discrimination, such as that based on skin color, religion or what country someone's mother came from.

*D*issent

Dissent—even disobedience under some conditions—is fundamental to American history, life and political philosophy. The United States was founded on dissent and civilized nations recognize that dissent should not be unduly suppressed.

Don't be afraid to disagree if you think someone or something is wrong. Perfection is quite rare in human endeavor.

"Where would we be today, where would the world be, if someone, sometime, somewhere, had not opposed 'organized' government? If you didn't learn it in school, begin a night school with yourself and learn now that everything that makes life worth living, everything that makes man's soul and body his own, everything that differs freedom from crushing despotism has been wrung from 'organized governments' by disobedience to the law."
— C.E.S. Wood[17]

Doubt

Doubt is necessary because people say and do things that are false, unclear, vague, intentionally obscure or incomplete.

You are not obligated to accept something as true merely because someone says it is.

Question things that don't make sense until you are satisfied with the answer or are ready to move on.

♪

"I doubt, therefore I think."
— Fernando Pessoa[18]

♪

"There is something wrong with questions that are supposed to be disposed of by answers. That is the trouble with the squares. They think that when you have answers you no longer have questions. And they want the greatest possible number of answers, the smallest number of questions. The ideal is to have no more questions. Then when you have no questions you have 'peace'."
— Thomas Merton[19]

$\mathcal{D}$*riving*

Driving a car is a useful skill. It is a serious matter. It is not something to do casually or under the wrong conditions.

Don't fiddle with your phone while driving. Really. See **Mortality**.

*E*ducation

Hold still while we educate you.

Education is what we used to call learning.

In the United States, learning is not valued highly except in certain limited situations in which it is demonstrably valuable in an instrumental, utilitarian or financial sense, to allow a person to perform a task that a different person wants performed.

By now you know that what you got out of high school was a mixed bag. **College** is likely to be the same, so plan ahead to get what you want and need.

"Honors high school texts are no more difficult than an eighth grade reader was before World War II."
    — Donald Hayes[20]

"I have no respect for any study whatsoever if its end is the making of money. Such studies are to me unworthy ones. They involve putting out of skills to hire, and are of value only insofar as they may develop the mind without occupying it for long."
    — Seneca[21]

♪

"A teacher soon discovers that there are only a few pupils whom he can help, many for whom he can do nothing except teach a few examination tricks, and a few to whom he can do nothing but harm."
— W. H. Auden[22]

♪

"I thought that even a society composed of well-trained ineducables might be improved by having a handful of educated persons sifted around in it every now and then."
— Albert Jay Nock[23]

♪

"An educated society is one that acts dispassionately, votes intelligently, respects cultural and literary excellence, rejects yahoos, abhors bigotry and admires scholarship. It perceives richness in leisure as well as in work, understands the past, transmits a sense of human decency and compassion to new generations ... and knows enough about freedom to protect it."
— Glenn Jackson[24]

$\mathcal{E}_{go}$

Sure, you're impressive. And attractive and charming. Go ahead, crank the Narcissus Knob as far as you like. So? What are you going to do with your life that is good or useful?

You can study yourself as much as you want to. Your own interests, grievances and physical self are undoubtedly a source of endless wonder to you. Don't assume anyone else will be as fascinated with you as you are.

Ego can be a useful driver toward laudable goals. It can also be a source of crude domineering behavior and gross indulgence in self-importance. You have seen this.

If all you are interested in is **Money** or Power, you can probably acquire them. Our society will reward you for having either. So what? Lily Tomlin reminded us that if you are ahead in the rat race, guess what, you're still a rat.

"The goal of discoverers is not to outdistance their peers but to transcend themselves. Hence individuals bent on real achievement should not waste too much of their time succeeding."
— Robert Grudin[25]

$\mathcal{E}$litism

Elitism is a key factor in the recognition of human differences. It simply means that we are capable of discerning among things or actions on a qualitative basis, and that we do not fear labeling the good differently from the bad.

Elitism is good in the right setting. It is necessary to the identification of quality, to the exercise of some kinds of **judgment** and to a commitment to truth even when most people support untruth or don't care about the difference.

There is nothing wrong with being an ordinary person living a good life. Ordinary people are not the "rabble" that some writers describe. That said, without a certain level of knowledge and experience, a person's ability to contribute in a significant way to the advancement of society is limited.

Recognize human differences without treating the less aware, the less educated or the less intelligent with discourtesy. At the same time, be aware that others with less knowledge or experience may look to you as an example or a leader. This is natural.

You know from your own experience that family income has an effect on a person's ability to do certain things and to have certain toys. You also know that this does not limit a person with **perseverance** from achieving high personal goals and goals recognized by society as having significant value. That's how you got where you are. Bravo.

♪

"The very essence of school is elitism. Schools exist to teach, to test, to rank hierarchically, to promote the idea that knowing and understanding more is better than knowing and understanding less. ... Civilization is elitist."
— William A. Henry[26]

♪

"I confess it disturbs me to see vulgar people. I find myself wondering what they do and where they live and whether they feel vulgar, and whether it would do any good to tell them how vulgar and useless they are, and how much better I should be without them."
— John Jay Chapman[27]

♪

"I never desired to please the rabble. What pleased them, I did not learn, and what I knew was far removed from their understanding."
— Epicurus[28]

♪

"The mass-man is he whose life lacks any purpose, and simply goes drifting along. Consequently, though his possibilities and his powers be enormous, he constructs nothing."
— José Ortega y Gasset[29]

Employment

That's right, a job. Unless you are wealthy, you will need one someday. Probably pretty soon.

Don't confuse your employment with your **work**.

Except for the wealthy, people work at jobs in order to have the life they want, or simply to eat.

How much job-work is **enough**? That depends on your need for **money** and how you choose to live.

Keep in mind that no one has a right to a job. What this really means in terms of social pain will become much more clear in your lifetime than it was in your parents' or grandparents' time. The economy is changing in ways that will require significant social adjustments.

$\mathcal{E}$*nemies*

There are people who will dislike or oppose you for reasons that are irrational.

Are they your enemies? Probably not. They just see things differently and want to do things their way. They may be opponents and they may be wrong, but are usually not enemies.

Sometimes you can find a way to work together on an issue of mutual interest with someone who is usually an opponent. Then you are a statesman !

Enough

In a society the economy of which is based on constant growth and constant change, we are taught by the example of friends, family and co-workers to always want more.

We are told that if we don't want more then there is something wrong with us.

We should think carefully about what our needs really are, bearing in mind that we live in a society that will not reward us for doing so.

How much is enough – for you?

♪

"I am the goldsmith of my chains!"
— Paul Valéry[30]

♪

"There is never enough "more."
— John Contreras[31]

♪

"For purposes of gain, we are inoculated with tastes and desires that have no roots in our deep physiological life but rather result from psychic or sensory stimuli deliberately inflicted."
— Paul Valéry[32]

$\mathcal{E}nvy$

So you'd like to be like that other person. You want what she or he has. You want to be adored that way. You want that life, free of burdens or stress.

That other person has burdens that you will never know. She has stresses that you cannot see. He has pain you will never feel.

They have stacks of toys. You don't have those toys.

But what you have, they don't. You have all the good that is in you, all the strength that is in you, all the creative energy that is in you. Most of all, you have kinds of happiness that are unique to you, that they will never have.

Live your way.

♪

"The kinds of happiness are not to be compared."
— Stephen Maturin (in a work of fiction by Patrick O'Brian)[33]

$\mathcal{E}$quality

Equality is one of the great buzzwords of recent generations. It is a large, sprawling word under which various interpretations and desires scuttle about, colliding and sending off sparks.

The crucial questions under the large tent of equality have to do with the distinction between equality of opportunity and equality of outcome. Most people agree that neither can be achieved with perfection or completeness. We disagree about what should be attempted and what our society's goals should be.

The largest area of agreement is that we should not arbitrarily prevent people from having opportunities to advance themselves as they choose.

You will encounter situations in which your own ideas and beliefs about equality are tested and changed. These are good learning opportunities.

"Behind all contemporary life lurks the provoking and profound injustice of the assumption that men are actually equal. Each move among men so obviously reveals the opposite that each move results in a painful clash. If this subject were broached in politics the passions would run too high to make oneself understood."
— José Ortega y Gasset[34]

♪

"...the field of struggle is not free and equal to all; that the mother earth, source of all wealth, is given by Special Privilege to a few; that society in general is taxed for a few; that the great economic forces and engines of society are monopolized by a few. And these Special Privileges, like so many conduit pipes, carry the wealth created by the many into the hands of the few beneficiaries of privilege."
— C.E.S. Wood[35]

♪

"A liberalism committed to equal opportunities must take into account the range of cultural beliefs and cultural commitments that are actually present in a given society ... . Having an opportunity to do X does not mean wanting to do X, but it does mean being able to do X without bearing excessive costs."
— David Miller[36]

Esthetics

You will develop your own esthetic sense—part of your **taste**. It will differ from that of other people.

Sometimes you will encounter things that are shockingly ugly or that just seem wrong. There are different ways to think about these horrors. They can be viewed as tangible evidence that in his youth, the Devil held a day job.

"An esthetic approach that declares nothing off limits in making artistic judgement can find itself saying everything about every thing, but nothing much about any thing. ... The demand for everything to be judged as equally valid—what we could call an imperative of relevance—means that cultural institutions which put the demands of access ahead of those of excellence, run the risk of ending up as nothing very special themselves: no longer willing to discriminate between in and out, the good, the bad and the ugly."
— Angus Kennedy[37]

43

$\mathcal{E}$thics

Congratulations, you have not been caught!

Yet.

If your standard of ethical behavior is that all is well because you have not yet been convicted of a crime, you're not worth much to society or to yourself.

Sometimes society will reward you for being ethical. Sometimes you will suffer for being ethical.

Who are you when no one is watching?

"Ethical behavior is doing the right thing when no one else is watching - even when doing the wrong thing is legal."
— Aldo Leopold[38]

$\mathcal{E}$*valuation*

Evaluation is not a substantive goal.

Evaluation is a process used to find out information about what a person knows, has done, has learned or for other purposes of determining a set of facts.

Pay careful attention to make sure that evaluation is really going to develop the useful information that it claims it will.

Excellence

We live in a society that pretends to value excellence, but in most cases does not.

A commitment to excellence is largely avoided in public schools because most parents don't want it. It is too much work and distracts from the casual slovenliness or simple workload of most people's daily life.

Excellence is abandoned by many people and at universities is discussed only by the less fearful faculty.

Excellence begins in each person's mind and ultimately can find support and solace only there.

From time to time there will be external support for your commitment to excellence. This support will often be counterbalanced by the opposition of those to whom excellence is always a threat. Phil Ochs spoke of this in his iconic song-poem *Crucifixion*, in which he wrote

> *But ignorance is everywhere and people have their way; success is an enemy to the losers of the day.*[39]

You will be conscious on a regular basis that you are in the presence of the losers of the day. They are everywhere. They are the social norm.

"If it were a question of fine roses, everyone knows that you must place a few of them under favorable conditions and cultivate them. You do not plant out seventy acres in roses

and then swear that they are the finest in the world because there are so many of them."
— John Jay Chapman[40]

♪

"...nobility is synonymous with a life of effort, ever set on excelling oneself, in passing beyond what one is to what one sets up as a duty and an obligation. In this way the noble life stands opposed to the common or the inert life, which reclines statically upon itself, compelled to perpetual immobility... ."
— José Ortega y Gasset[41]

Expertise

Expertise is valuable. We need experts to design aircraft so they fly, build bridges so they stay upright and purify water so we can drink it. You can think of many other examples.

Who is an expert? Any of us can declare ourself to be an expert in anything we choose. However, we must then be able to demonstrate that we really are, through acts and decisions.

Most of us are not experts in more than one or two things.

Respect for expertise is necessary, but it can be overdone. Do not be afraid to question expertise when you think an expert is mistaken, but have your own facts properly arrayed to do so.

Mere disagreement without a rationale is rarely useful. We need **thinking**.

"Specialized excellence has two dangers: that we will use it as a means of ignoring our own weak areas, and that specialized society will offer us excessive rewards for it, yoking us to plow a thin furrow."
— Robert Grudin[42]

♪

"The sovereignty of the unqualified individual, of the human being as such, generically, has now passed from being a juridical idea or ideal to be a psychological state inherent in the average man."

— José Ortega y Gasset [43]

$\mathcal{F}_{ear}$

Many people go through life in a constant state of fear. In some cases this is because they do not have **enough** of what they deem necessary, particularly **money**. That fear is rational in a society like ours in which money has value but people, on the whole, do not.

People also fear being different because being different can lead to physical harm, social rejection and limited opportunities. That, too, is a rational fear because our society, particularly in certain regional **culture**s, expects conformity of opinion and action.

Social and professional punishment is common, widespread and ordinary. It will happen to you. Move on—or fight if you need to—when it does.

$\mathcal{F}$*ocus*

Remaining focused on what you want to do and on things of value to you is one of the most difficult tasks in life. Life will provide as many distractions as it can. Distraction is a modern social norm; everything about advertising and much of social media is designed to distract you from what you were doing.

It is very difficult to focus in college, because you will be surrounded with so many opportunities to do new and interesting things with attractive and interesting people. That is fine up to a point—after all, college is a place to try new things. Learn where the proper boundary is between exploration and focus.

"Even if you had a large part of your life remaining before you, you would have to organize it very economically to have enough for all the things that are necessary; as things are, isn't it the height of folly to learn inessential things when time's so short?"
— Seneca[44]

"If a man is employed, earns his living, and can devote but an hour a day to reading, at home or in the bus or the subway, his hour is taken up with crime stories, nonsense, tittle-tattle and invariably the same 'news', in a confusion and abundance that seem calculated to bewilder and stultify people's minds."
— Paul Valéry[45]

♪

"If there is to be an alternative to the culture of distraction, it can only be created one family at a time, by parents and citizens determined to preserve a saving remnant of those who prize memory and true learning above all else. Adult self-control, not digital parental controls, is the chief requirement for the transmittal of individual and historical memory. ... The endless warnings about the dangers of too much screen time for the young evade the fact that children are simply following in their parents' footsteps—or, more to the point, sinking into the spreading round indentations their parents have left on the couch."
 — Susan Jacoby[46]

♪

"Without the ability to direct our attention where we will, we become more receptive to those who would direct our attention where they will."
 — Matthew Crawford[47]

$\mathcal{F}$reedom

We take many freedoms for granted. Be glad for those freedoms, but don't think that they all happened by accident. They required many sacrifices and a willingness to take risks by many people who came before us. You may be called upon to do your part for future generations.

♪

"In Europe, charters of liberty have been granted by power. America has set the example . . . of charters of power granted by liberty."
— James Madison[48]

♪

"If freedom had always had to rely on governments to encourage her growth she would probably be still in her infancy or else definitively buried with the inscription 'another angel in heaven.' ... freedom is not the answer to everything, and it has frontiers. The freedom of each finds its limits in that of others; no one has a right to absolute freedom. The limit where freedom begins and ends, where its rights and duties come together, is called law, and the State itself must bow to the law."
— Albert Camus[49]

$\mathcal{F}$riendship

Friendship is the greatest of all human relationships.

Your friends are the people who are *still there* when you are fired from your job.

They are *still there* when you are roasted in the news media.

They are *still there* when you are, rightly or wrongly, in jail.

You'll be surprised at how few there really are and who they are. They won't necessarily be the people you expect.

A good friend is invaluable. A friend tells you the truth (with **kindness**) when you don't want to hear it, supports you when you are down and stands with you when you are everyone else's target.

Your friends are *still there* even after you dump on them and trash them (but you'd better **apologize**).

"When the mere chance that causes two men to meet, take stock of one another, gauge one another, etc., changes imperceptibly into a kind of necessity, an event that couldn't not have been, that justification *(in the evangelical sense) of an accidental case is: friendship. Friends are these two men who* saved *from chance and accident an occurrence that was*

54

commonplace and that very likely would have fallen, such as it was, into the statistics of the molecular shocks of mankind."
— Paul Valéry[50]

"Friends are not concerned with what might be made of one another, but only with the enjoyment of one another; and the condition of this enjoyment is a ready acceptance of what is and the absence of any desire to change or to improve. A friend is not somebody one trusts to behave in a certain manner, who supplies certain wants, who has certain useful abilities, who possesses certain merely agreeable qualities, or who holds certain acceptable opinions."
— Michael Oakeshott[51]

"I am sensible that, according to the past experience of mankind, friendship is the chief joy of human life … ."
— David Hume[52]

Groups

People are generally social beings and enjoy doing things in groups. Try a new group now and then.

Don't stay in a group if the only reason is ritual or mechanical habit. This is social necrophilia: the practice of continuing to do something with other people long after the activity is dead to you. Move on when this happens.

Do not agree with a group if what it says or does is wrong. Follow instead the honorable example of Aristides de Sousa Mendes, the Portuguese consul who disobeyed his own government to issue thousands of visas to Jews and others seeking to flee the Nazis in 1940. Denied his pension and any useful employment after this, he died in poverty.

"I could not have acted otherwise, and I therefore accept all that has befallen me with love."
— Aristides de Sousa Mendes[53]

"You shall not follow a majority in wrongdoing."
— Exodus 23:2

ℋome

There are places that always feel like home. You feel right when you are there. There are familiar good things to see and do. The smells are homey. The climate feels right.

These places may be your actual home, or they may be special places that you go where you always feel at home, welcomed by the very air.

There are also homes that are fictional and yet so perfectly natural for you that you want to be there. Think about what makes those places seem so good and go about building those good things into your real home life.

"I am sorry, Uncle Joseph, but I am going back to Islandia to live the rest of my life."
> — John Lang, in a work of fiction by Austin Tappan Wright[54]

ℋonesty

If you are within sight of the truth, you know where to go.

Sometimes things that appear true contain trace amounts of nonsense that need to be removed. Our natural tendency is to find some small sheltering corner in which we can add a caveat, a weasel-word or a fuzzing over that allows us to be not-quite-honest.

You must decide for yourself when kindness suggests that the edges of the truth be softened.

Society is full of "truth vendors," each offering their own version of the truth.[55]

Sometimes you will be in a situation in which telling the truth will make people unhappy, yet you must tell the truth. This is part of life, though it can be painful.

"I hate to give offense, yet there are times when not to offend is unrighteous."
— C.E.S. Wood [56]

"True propositions are those that are good to believe, and that correctly portray the world as it is. This is truth's job description, as it were. Beliefs or propositions are true when they do that job."
— Michael P. Lynch[57]

Hope

Hope is a good thing to have, but if it is not to lead to disappointment, it needs to be based in a certain level of realism.

Hoping for something to happen when you have not done what is necessary to make it happen or increase the likelihood of it happening is simply laziness coated in candy. Sure, you might get lucky. This time.

Hoping for something for which there is no reasonable likelihood, or for which there is no supporting evidence, is something you are free to do, but don't burden other people with it.

$\mathcal{I}$mprovisation

If it were not for the patterns in life, improvisations would not be noticed.

Some kind of foundation or pattern is very helpful in almost all aspects of life. When that is laid down, improvisation becomes the frosting.

"I was especially struck by your remark that the charm of good music is that it surprises the ear by the unexpected interval, and that the element of surprise is permanent, no matter how familiar the music may become. It is a principle which carries over into other affairs of life; what we crave is the element of freshness, and some of the most vivid experiences seem to have in them an element of freshness which is perpetual."
— Alfred North Whitehead[58]

Individualism

Individualism is one side of the scale upon the other side of which is society. We all decide where we belong on this scale.

Sometimes our position changes under different circumstances. Our need for other people varies over time. Our desire for freedom from social norms may be very strong at one point in our lives and weaker at another point.

Individualism is not a shrine or a defensive position, it is one end of a balance.

"You should neither become like the bad because they are many, nor be an enemy of the many because they are unlike you. Retire into yourself as much as you can."
— Seneca[59]

"Civilization is before all, the will to live in common. A man is uncivilized, barbarian in the degree in which he does not take others into account."
— José Ortega y Gasset[60]

Joy

Joy is available in small things as well as in the large issues of life. Sometimes finding a small bit of happiness in an obscure corner can break the spell of sadness or take the edge off of depression.

Turning that corner is a short distance in a short time, but the difference between sliding downhill and striding uphill is not that great on the ground. Let the small joys help you achieve the great ones.

"I believe we are creatures destined for joy who regularly rob ourselves of it because we are taught that there is some reason we shouldn't have it. The strange part is that we believe the teaching."
— John Contreras[61]

Judgment

You will be told not to judge, that to exercise judgment is bad and that to apply your standards to another person's actions using judgment is wrong.

This social norm misunderstands the nature of judgment. Judgment is necessary to **excellence**. It is necessary to **honesty**.

Judgment is an important escort of truth.

"Substituting rules for judgment starts a self-defeating cycle, since judgment can only be developed by using it."
— Dee Hock[62]

Kindness

Kindness should be the way we normally treat all other people, as well as those animals that come under our care.

We cannot always be kind because sometimes our commitment to honesty requires that the truth be spoken out loud or put in writing. The truth can be hurtful, but present it with kindness when you can.

A compliment is almost always well received and rarely does any harm.

*L*ove

Young love is untempered iron. It is still warm from the forging. It is strong but brittle. The breaking process can release extraordinary emotional outwashes. Know this ahead of time – know that you will survive, love and flourish again.

Mature love is a great river flowing; it feels inevitable, constant and multidimensional.

In between comes the complexity of developing love. It seems to have more dimensions on the inside than on the outside.

Love is not the same as desire or **lust** or liking or **friendship**, but it can overlap with and incorporate these things.

$\mathcal{L}$ust

Lust is natural and is part of being human. We should not fear it or run from it or call it a bad thing.

Lust can be a factor in good **sex** and, in its nonsexual aspects, it can lead to positive achievements.

However, lust is hard to manage or control and can result in doing things that are stupid, harmful to others or generally destructive.

It is hard to think clearly while influenced by lust. Slow down and try anyway. Sometimes lust leads to love, the "golden conversion."[63]

Money

You will need enough money to exist and ideally thrive in our society, which values only money and fame. Our society will throw you away without even noticing if you are not economically viable.

Without a certain level of financial capacity you are unfortunately not a real citizen in our country. You are part of the soil, fit only for bootprints.

How much money is **enough**? That depends on who you are.

Learning how money works is a necessary part of citizenship, whether you like it or not. No matter how much of it you need, learn how to achieve that goal.

Other people, including your **friends**, will offer to use your money for their own needs. Helping others is a virtue, but most of us cannot afford to be drained of money by others. Help when you can, but preserve your own financial viability.

"Society pays only for the services it sees."
— Henri Beyle[64]

Mortality

Mortality sounds nicer than death.

We don't like to talk about death. Fear of death is natural. Having experienced sensation, we naturally want to continue doing so, despite Epicurus's matter-of-fact assertion that there is "nothing terrible in not living."[65] Yet we recognize that we cannot live our accustomed life of sensation forever.

Even those who imagine an afterlife rarely assume that it will resemble how we function while alive.

We are all ghosts most of the time.

We were not here a hundred years ago and we will not be here a hundred years from now.

Where we were prior to our birth is hardly discussed, yet where we go after life is a subject of constant speculation and concern despite the fact that the two states, viewed abstractly, have much in common.

Do some good while you are here in the flesh. Have some fun while you are here, too. Death will come in good time, there is no need to seek it out.

"Imagine you were now dead, or had not lived before this moment. Now view the rest of your life as a bonus, and live as nature directs. You may leave this life at any moment: have this possibility in mind in all that you do or say or think."
— Marcus Aurelius[66]

♪

"The vast majority are so dead while they live that one may suppose that they stay dead when they die."
                    — Albert Jay Nock[67]

♪

"Life is never incomplete if it is an honorable one.   At whatever point you leave life, if you leave it in the right way, it is a whole."
                    — Seneca[68]

Music

Playing the instrument is not the same as playing the music.

Technique is necessary to music but if there is no music in you, playing the instrument well won't produce any.

Life without music is a partial, flat and exsanguinated life. Keep music in your life.

See also **Improvisation**.

$\mathcal{N}$ationhood

Nation-states come into being for many reasons. Such nations exist because they are strong enough to do so, because no stronger nation wants their land and resources or because social and political norms prevent stronger nations from devouring weaker ones.

No nation has an inherent right to exist, though it may have strong ethical arguments for its existence.

Nations are made up of people and in many cases these people have a similar **Culture**. Nations containing many varied cultures are less stable and more prone to internal conflict than those containing one core culture.

O*pinions*

We all have opinions. They are based on what we have experienced, what we have been told and what has sifted into our minds with the dust of daily life.

Sometimes we spend too much time standing in the shadow of our own opinions and refusing to get into the sunlight of other people's ideas.

♪

"Always remember, the other guy may be right."
— C.E.S. Wood[69]

♪

"… I do not want to be narrow-minded. I heard recently of a man so narrow-minded that a mosquito could stand on the bridge of his nose and kick him in both eyes at once."
— Levi Pennington[70]

$\mathcal{P}$atience

Patience isn't easy for anyone, and it is especially hard for a young person. You are surrounded by people who have all kinds of nice toys and appear to live a bit easier than you do, and you naturally want to start doing the same Right Now.

Keep in mind that the things, results, friends, lovers and feelings that you want Right Now have a way of making life extremely complicated: you juggle them until they all land on you at once and you are sitting on your tail in the mud.

One way to make your desires for Right Now work for you is to plan ahead a bit so you can see that Yes, goals are visible and achievable and are really no great way off.

Patience is for planning.

$\mathcal{P}_{eace}$

What is peace? It is not the absence of war, that is too narrow a notion. There are dozens of things that cause our lives to be less than peaceful, yet we do not call them war.

Things like anger, stress, illness and poverty are examples of obstacles to peace in our daily existence.

Peace is necessary to your attaining a reasonable level of **autonomy**.

"Obviously one does not want to inflict death and wounds if it can be avoided, but I cannot feel that mere killing is all-important. We shall all be dead in less than a hundred years, and most of us by the sordid horror called 'natural death.' The truly evil thing is to act in such a way that peaceful life becomes impossible. War damages the fabric of civilization not by the destruction it causes (the net effect of a war may even be to increase the productive capacity of the world as a whole), nor even by the slaughter of human beings, but by stimulating hatred and dishonesty."
      — George Orwell[71]

*P*erfection

You're not perfect? Good heavens, how are we to deal with this?

Humanity is imperfectible. This is not well understood by people who develop systems for the perfect society. You'll meet them.

Maybe you have had a perfect upbringing in which everything you needed was taken care of and nobody ever said nasty things to you.

That's over.

You will now be faced each day with people who have problems. Yeah, they are imperfect. And guess what, you will sometimes have to deal with that because— guess what—you're not a kid anymore.

If you have not had to build or use your own capacity to deal with bad situations, the transition may be tough for you. Keep in mind that it is normal. It isn't something wrong with *you*, it is a part of growing up and learning how to live in a messy world.

You'll do just fine.

"The real question you are asking is whether what we want from society is for it to protect us or perfect us."
— "Plato" (as conceived by Rebecca Newberger Goldstein)[72]

♪

"You have this strength inside yourself. And if you stay true to that voice that clearly knows what's right and what's wrong, sometimes you're going to mess up, but you can steer back and keep going."
— Barack Obama[73]

$\mathcal{P}$erseverance

Perseverance is **patience** clothed in mail and sword.

Perseverance is **focused** determination.

Perseverance is the single greatest factor affecting individual **success**, whatever we conceive success to be.

Perseverance often involves hard work, but it is not the same thing. Perseverance means never giving up on things that need to be done.

Good **judgment** helps determine what is worth pursuing with perseverance and what is not.

*P*olitics

Politics requires compromise to be effective over time as the basis for government. Government without compromise tends to become ideologically fixed and rigid, impervious to new ideas. It can also become a tyranny of the majority, simply legalized force.

The compromise needed in politics necessarily represents the triumph of adequacy over **excellence**. This is nothing new. However, it is not well-understood that because compromise usually precludes excellence, we can rarely expect excellence from any government entity. Government entities operate based on the need for *adequacy*.

Some politicians have a genuine philosophy and have gone into public service to accomplish something. Others are deciduous: they shed and replace their beliefs as needed and are only interested in themselves.

"The political man, to a degree far greater than any other, must be responsive to the wills of others. Indeed, if he is to win votes, he must be an ideological weathervane, pointing in the direction of the strongest wind. ... Such a man could no longer be true to himself, he was trying to go to heaven with a party."
  — Robert M. Crunden[74]

♪

"Every time I hear a political speech or I read those of our leaders, I am horrified at having, for years, heard nothing which sounded human. It is always the same words telling the same lies. And the fact that men accept this, that the people's anger has not destroyed these hollow clowns, strikes me as proof that men attribute no importance to the way they are governed; that they gamble—yes, gamble—with a whole part of their life and their so-called 'vital interests'."

— Albert Camus [75]

$\mathcal{P}$*opulation*

The world already contains too many people.

A certain proportion of people now alive or being born are and will always be superfluous. They cannot feed or shelter themselves and no one will need them to perform any tasks in exchange for money, food or shelter. Society has no idea what to do with such people. They represent a permanent underclass trapped not only in poverty but without hope or purpose.

It is impossible to preserve a functioning biological space for long-term sustainable use by people without limiting human population.

What methods of reducing the human population are just and morally acceptable?

Only by working toward a goal of a smaller human population can humanity have a good future. This will require significant changes in social, economic and religious norms.

There is reason for pessimism about the outcome.

"It still remains unrecognized, that to bring a child into existence without a fair prospect of being able, not only to provide food for its body, but instruction and training for its mind, is a moral crime, both against the unfortunate offspring and against society ... "
— John Stuart Mill[76]

♪

"... in the 21st century, there is a good chance that most humans will lose ... their military and economic value. ... The age of the masses is over. ... Maybe the biggest question of 21st century economics is what will be the need in the economy for most people in the year 2050. The biggest question maybe in economics and politics of the coming decades will be what to do with all these useless people."
    — Yuval Noah Harari[77]

$\mathcal{P}$*ride*

Pride is appropriate in modest doses. You should take pride in your work when it is done well.

Pride can get out of control more easily than you think. Don't turn your back on it.

$\mathcal{P}$*rivacy*

We live in a society in which thousands of people are paid each day to find out things about you. Some of them work for your governments. Some of them work for private business. Some of them work for nonprofit entities. A few of them even work for somebody else's government.

True privacy is all but impossible. However, you can take steps to limit what all of these vampires get from you and what use they make of it. Avoid putting factual information about yourself into any public electronic venue. Make slight changes to that information when doing so is legal and does not harm your own interests.

For example, there are occasions on which you can put slightly different birthdays, slightly different spellings of your name, slightly different details about yourself into a form that electronic trawlers might find. Have fun !

"From now, know that every border you cross, every purchase you make, every call you dial, every cell phone tower you pass, friend you keep, article you write, site you visit, subject line you type, and packet you route, is in the hands of a system whose reach is unlimited but whose safeguards are not."
— Edward Snowden[78]

"There is no greater joy than to live alone and unknown."
— Albert Camus[79]

$\mathcal{P}$romises

Promises are a serious matter. Do not lightly make a promise.

Do not promise what you cannot deliver.

Sometimes you will make someone unhappy by refusing to make a promise you cannot keep. That is better than failing to deliver on the promise or harming yourself in the process of keeping a promise that should not have been made.

ℛarity

We all tend to place a higher value on things that are exotic, unavailable and uncommon. We don't appreciate the remarkable beauty and variety to be found right under our noses each day.

"The temptations that come to conscientious observers are common to humanity, and one of the subtlest is to undervalue what is at hand and overvalue the rare or distant."
— Florence Merriam Bailey[80]

Reason

Reason is the application of *rational* **thinking** to a set of facts or ideas. It is necessary to use reason when knowing the truth is important.

We live in a society in which actions by the government are required to be reasonable yet many are not, and in which actions by private people are not required to be reasonable, yet many are.

Reason is how we get through life's decision-making processes. Without it we would accomplish nothing.

♪

"Do you possess reason?"
"I do."
"Why not use it then? With reason doing its job, what else do you want?"
      — Marcus Aurelius[81]

♪

"Reliance upon reason ... assumes a certain community of interest and outlook between oneself and one's audience. ... As the political constituency grows larger and more heterogeneous, the appeal to reason becomes more difficult, since there are fewer universally conceded assumptions from which agreement can start."
      — Bertrand Russell[82]

♪

"There are two equally dangerous extremes, to shut reason out, and to let nothing else in."
— Blaise Pascal[83]

♪

"Finally ... I come to what may be called respect for truth, or the Socratic spirit, or intellectual integrity, or a determination to follow the argument whither it may lead. This essential element in our civilization has never been particularly strong: it was decaying rapidly in the late thirties: but the pace is now accelerating, even among educated people, to a quite disastrous degree."
— Victor Gollancz[84]

Religion

Religion plays a significant role in many people's lives. What that role is varies widely and how people live their faith in daily life is as varied as there are differences in people.

If you choose to promote your religion to those who do not share it, consider what aspects of your faith are most likely to be attractive to another person.

No one wants to be told what to do according to the precepts of a religious faith that they do not hold. Using faith as a club to beat the unfaithful is not a good way to demonstrate that your faith is one to share.

A faith that requires coercion to compel people to behave as though they shared a faith that in fact they do not is a weak, desperate faith.

Show by example. Give your faith a good name—don't assume that it has one already.

Never assume that only those of your faith are capable of doing good. There is surely room in the world for more good, whatever its source.

"If the church ... says it enters politics and violates my freedom for the good of others, I answer; that has been the everlasting cause of hell upon earth. ..."
— C.E.S. Wood[85]

♪

"More tears were shed over prayers that were granted than ever were shed over prayers that were refused."
— attributed to Saint Teresa of Avila (in a work of fiction by Patrick O'Brian)[86]

♪

"If, to outgrow nihilism, one must return to Christianity, one may well follow the impulse and outgrow Christianity in Hellenism."
— Albert Camus[87]

♪

"Paganism for oneself, Christianity for others is the instinctive desire of each person."
— Albert Camus[88]

Reputation

Your reputation is what other people think of you. It may or may not reflect who you really are. You can influence your reputation but you cannot control it.

It is not the same as your **character**.

♪

"Bad reputations are easier to bear than good ones, for the good ones are heavy to drag along; one has to prove oneself always up to it and any lapse is looked upon as a crime. With bad reputations, a lapse is to your credit."
— Albert Camus[89]

Revenge

Other people will sometimes treat you badly. You may be left in the mud in the ditch as they stroll off laughing at you.

Anger and a desire for revenge are natural in this situation. They will inflame you in the short term. Allow this flame to burn bright and briefly and be gone, for all it can burn is you.

♪

"For as for the first wrong, it doth but offend the law, but the revenge of that wrong putteth the law out of office."
— Francis Bacon[90]

♪

"Living well is the best revenge."
— George Herbert[91]

♪

"Those with good sense are slow to anger, and it is their glory to overlook an offense."
— Proverbs 19:11

$\mathcal{R}$*isks*

Q: Don't you live life pretty close to the edge?

A: That depends on where you think the edge is.

♪

"You cannot create experience. You must undergo it."
— Albert Camus[92]

S*ameness*

We live in a society that rewards sameness. The more you live and behave just like the neighbors, the easier it is to get along in life.

How boring.

S*cience*

Science is a process, not a result. George Orwell described it as "a method of thought which obtains verifiable results by reasoning logically from observed fact."[93]

There is no place for immobile opinions in science, because science is necessarily responsive to facts. New facts appear all the time. In other words, what can't be wrong can't be science.

Science is unlikely to explain everything because the universe is hard to understand in its complexity.

Science, and a respect for science, is crucial to our survival in the world but it is not all of our world.

"Our means of investigation and action have far outstripped our means of representation and understanding."
— Paul Valéry[94]

"Fully 42 percent say that all living things, including humans, have existed in their present form since the beginning of time. This level of scientific ignorance cannot be blamed solely on religious fundamentalism, because the proportion of Americans who reject evolution is higher — by 15 percentage points — than the proportion who believe in a literal interpretation of the Bible. Something else must be at work, and that something else is the low level of science education in

American elementary and secondary schools, as well as in many community colleges."
— Susan Jacoby[95]

"To fall in love with the impersonal beauty of objectivity, which doesn't love us back, is moral achievement in itself."
— Rebecca Newberger Goldstein[96]

Selfishness

Selfishness as we think of it today is always seen as uniformly bad. Consider instead the nuanced view of selfishness espoused by C.E.S. Wood:

Pay a *just* attention to others.

Maintain your *essential* duty to yourself.

View selfishness as that duty to yourself.

Keep it balanced with your duty to others.

♪

"Be more selfish—your life was given to you to live. Live it. Draw the line between a just attention to others and your essential duty to yourself. Let living be reciprocal."
— C.E.S. Wood[97]

*S*ex

Sex is fun. But you know that already. Sex can be a source of great intimacy with the right person. However, sex is not *important*. It is not love. It is not all there is to intimacy, even physical intimacy. Sometimes what your partner wants is a good back rub or just some cuddle time.

The relationship of love and sexual **lust** is genuine, but it is a relationship, not a shared identity. Never base a long-term relationship primarily on sexual desire.

In college you may hear lectures by well-meaning third-string bureaucrats informing you that you should not have sex with another person unless that person signs a release two days in advance and gives a copy to the Dean. Ignore this nonsense.

Don't let your basic humanity be smothered by nervous officials who know nothing of how life should be lived. If the time is right and your partner is willing, by all means *carpe denim*.[98]

"The mistake we have made throughout the ages has been to load onto sex the incubus of success or failure of marriage, to look upon sex as a resolution, *an ending. In reality it offers us, if we could only see it, a fresh* beginning *every time in that relationship of which it is a part."*
— Mary S. Calderone[99]

♪

[Advice at a training session]

"Do not make unwanted sexual advances."

Someone demanded querulously from the back, "But how do you know they're unwanted until you try?" (OK, it was me.)

"Do you really want me to answer that?" he finally responded, trying to make a joke out of it. I did want him to answer, because it's something I'd been wondering—how are you supposed to know in advance? Do people wear their desires emblazoned on their foreheads?"
    — Laura Kipnis[100]

*S*ilence

There are times when maintaining a discreet silence is the best thing to do. Even if speaking or writing about something would gratify your ego—or result in a different outcome—it is still sometimes better to be silent.

You know things that you have wisely chosen to keep to yourself because your good **judgment** tells you that this is the best thing to do.

If you speak, you may find yourself "volunteered" for something that you don't want to do and that will cause you to lose your **focus**.

Sometimes by remaining silent you learn all kinds of things that you would not have found out if you were being noisy.

"No one has taught her the immense value of silence."
> — Stephen Maturin (in a work of fiction by Patrick O'Brian)[101]

"The benefits of silence are off the books. They are not measured in the gross domestic product, yet the availability of silence surely contributes to creativity and innovation. They do not show up explicitly in social statistics such as level of educational achievement, yet one consumes a great deal of silence in the course of becoming educated."
> — Matthew B. Crawford[102]

S*olitude*

We live in a society of noisy humans. It is increasingly hard to find true quiet time, private time in sufficient quantity to allow your mind to shed some of the goo that builds up in daily life.

Sometimes you will need this solitude in which to think about some particular thing—a personal problem, a project, a relationship, a choice to be made.

Other times you want that time in order to reconnect with the natural world of which we are all a part.

Never hesitate to arrange for periods of solitude, put them on your calendar and make them stick.

♪

"It is, it seems, a social crime to desire solitude."
    — Jean Cocteau[103]

$Speed$

Ours is a society increasingly based on going fast. We do things quickly and we expect our equipment, our friends and our family members to do things quickly, too.

Speed is not a virtue in itself. Whether it is a virtue in a given situation depends on the situation.

Sometimes going fast is necessary. Fire engines and aircraft need to go fast much of the time in order to perform their duties. So does the Internet, to achieve its technical functionality.

Speed can be misapplied to situations in which more careful action or contemplation is best: running fast to escape the inside of a torus serves no purpose.

Learn to distinguish situations in which speed is needed from those in which it is used or expected inappropriately.

One example of the role of speed in our daily lives is in the economy:

"There are only three ways markets can expand to keep the economy growing: spatially—build new factories and open new stores in new places; differentially—create an endless variety of new products for consumers to buy; and temporally—accelerate the product cycle. When spatial expansion and differential production reach their limits, the most efficient and effective strategy for promoting growth is to increase the speed of product churn. In fast food, fast fashion, fast networks, and fast markets, time has become money in

ways Benjamin Franklin never could have anticipated. … Out with the old and in with the new, and the faster the better."
— Mark C. Taylor[104]

Standards

Standards are necessary in order to have **excellence**. People uninterested in quality always argue against standards.

Standards can be easy to establish: "airplanes must be capable of sustained flight." However, many standards are difficult to establish. This is usually due to disagreement or misunderstanding over the goal to be achieved by having standards, but can also result from technical problems in measurement or definitions.

There are many kinds of standards. Some are societal, some are technical, some, such as esthetic standards, are largely personal or are influenced by those you respect or whose knowledge or experience you value.

Be careful in establishing and applying standards, but do not be afraid to do so.

"Good qualities are easier to destroy than bad ones, and therefore uniformity is most easily achieved by lowering all standards."
> — Bertrand Russell[105]

"The conditions of modern life tend inevitably, implacably, to make individuals all alike, to level character; and, unhappily yet necessarily, the average tends to decline toward the lowest type.*"*
> — Paul Valéry[106]

$Study$

Studying should be fun. We all have things we'd like to know more about, whether it is Greek history, the mechanics of railroad engines or the best places to find a trout. All of these involve study.

Scholarship is study taken to its logical end in terms of thoroughness and detail. Its value extends beyond the needs of the student and encompasses other people's potential interest.

♪

"A scholar's real audience is not yet born. A scholar must build for the future, not the present."
— Camille Paglia[107]

♪

"We ought not to be embarrassed of appreciating the truth and of obtaining it wherever it comes from, even if it comes from races distant and nations different from us. Nothing should be dearer to the seeker of truth than the truth itself, and there is no deterioration of the truth, nor belittling either of one who speaks it or conveys it."
— Abu Yousuf Yaqub ibn Ishaq al-Kindi[108]

♪

"The first motive which ought to impel us to study is the desire to augment the excellence of our nature, and to render an intelligent being yet more intelligent."
— Montesquieu[109]

S*tupidity*

Some people are stupid. We don't like to talk about this. Some people deny that it is true.

Some people who are not generally stupid have blind spots that they can't seem to think their way through.

When you encounter stupidity in daily life, accept it as what it is and work around it as you would work around any other immovable obstacle.

"[By] the 1960s … we had reached the point where virtually all smart youngsters were going to college. Only the stupid or the poor were not going on to college."
— Daniel Patrick Moynihan [110]

"We can do little about the stupid except to hope that they decrease in number though socially acceptable means …"
— Alan Contreras [111]

*S*uccess

Success means achieving what you want to in life. It has nothing to do with money, power or toys.

Your goals may change over time and you will undoubtedly need to adjust what you do. This will affect what your idea of success is.

$\mathcal{T}$*aste*

Taste is part of the family of ideas and concepts that includes **standards, judgment** and **discrimination**. It is the most complex of these because it includes two primary notions cohabiting under the same word.

First, there is the question of taste as a partial synonym for judgment and discrimination. This usage assumes a limited corridor of "acceptable" taste, sometimes called "good taste," outside which lies the wasteland of "bad taste," a locale in which no one wants to be discovered. This usage is problematic because it blends into the social norms that we call customs, manners and decorum, and includes expectations of purely personal preferences in the fine arts and in lifestyles that are in essence arbitrary.

There is also the more useful meaning, which is your personal taste. What you like and prefer in music, clothing, books, art and other aspects of life constitutes your taste.

Having good taste is not a crime.

$\mathcal{T}$*elevision*

Television is one of the least useful inventions of the past hundred years. Although it has some crude utility, its net effect on society has been largely negative. It encourages people to avoid each other and stare at silliness for hours. It is wholly unnecessary to a good life.

Live without one.

♪

"I have never seen TV, that is never watched it. Once when I did happen to pass in front of a set I saw the commercial that was on: two little figures were dancing around worshipping a roll of toilet paper, chanting a hymn in its honor. I think this is symbolic enough, isn't it?"
— Thomas Merton [112]

$\mathcal{T}hanks$

"Thanks" is one of the most underutilized words in our daily life. It is also one of the most helpful. It is almost always appropriate to say "thank you."

Thankfulness is also a larger concept applicable to our broader existence. Even on bad days, it doesn't take long to think of reasons to be thankful.

$\mathcal{T}$ hinking

Having an opinion is not the same as thinking.

Feelings are not thoughts.

Thinking is something that we learn very early in life, but sometimes we get out of the habit or we only think about certain things.

There is no reason to analyze every aspect of life all the time, but thinking is necessary on many occasions and in a wide variety of contexts. Don't confuse thinking with other kinds of mental activity.

Learn how to be a careful, critical thinker and keep that skill always available to use when it is needed.

"It is not good enough to have a point of view ... what we need is thoughts." [113]
— Michael Oakeshott

"To be surprised, to wonder, is to begin to understand. This is the sport, the luxury, special to the intellectual man."
— José Ortega y Gasset[114]

"The opportunity or the necessity of rewarding the mind, in the guise of certain individuals, with a definite place in the social structure has in every age raised a fundamental difficulty which by its nature cannot be overcome. It lies not only in making the right definition but also in being obliged to make inevitable judgments of quality. *At every attempt, we come against the insoluble question of* gauging the best.*"*
— Paul Valéry[115]

♪

"The ideal of serious enjoyment of what isn't instantly understood is rare in American life. It is under constant siege. It is the object of scorn from both the left and the right. The pleasures of critical thinking ought not to be seen as belonging to the province of an elite. They are the birthright of every citizen. For such pleasures are at the very heart of literacy, without which democracy itself is dulled."
— Steve Wasserman[116]

$\mathcal{V}$alues

We all have values. These values differ. That is all right, so long as we recognize that values are inherently personal and cannot be imposed on someone else.

We start out with values from our family, adjust our values based on what we see and hear in the world and eventually develop our own value pattern that we share with others either intentionally or through the example of how we live our life.

There are also larger values based in our **culture** that occupy a different space.

You may need to look around to determine your comfort level in different aspects of life as your values expand and change, which they will.

It is always hard to live in a community whose underlying values differ significantly from your own.

$\mathcal{V}$ulgarity

Vulgar simply means common, in the sense of the common people, everyday words and so on.

Vulgar language is common language used by the broad community of people. It may or may not include foul or crude language. It is the language that we hear every day in supermarkets, bus stops, auto repair shops, parking lots and fast food restaurants. It has its place.

$\mathcal{W}$*inning*

Winning feels good. Sometimes winning is important, when you win for an idea, not just for your ego.

Win fair. Victory at the cost of veracity is not winning, it is cheating.

$\mathcal{W}_{ork}$

Your work is not quite the same as your **employment**. Your *work* is what you want to do or feel called to do.

Work, properly conceived, should be a pleasure. Build your life so that each work day is something to look forward to.

"The goal of everyone is how to live without working. To do this one must either have inherited or stolen money, or one must persuade society to pay one for doing what one likes, i.e., for playing."
— W.H. Auden[117]

"I want to say, in all seriousness, that a great deal of harm is being done in the modern world by belief in the virtuousness of work, and that the road to happiness and prosperity lies in the organized diminution of work."
— Bertrand Russell[118]

"By [a passion for work] I do not mean the passionate longing for some as-yet-unwon goal, but rather the delight of being totally within one's element—of identifying fully with one's work and seeing it as an expression of one's own character."
— Robert Grudin[119]

♪

"The collective effort until this moment, and the collective delusion until this moment, has been precisely my illusion when I was a little boy: that you could get what you wanted, and become what you said you were going to be, painlessly."
— James Baldwin[120]

♪

"What sordid misery there is in the condition of a man who works and in a civilization based on men who work. ... People talk a lot nowadays about the dignity of work, and about the need for it. But it's a fraud. There is dignity in work only when it is work freely accepted."
— Albert Camus[121]

Υ*outh*

Lost youth is the only kind.

♪

"At sixteen, we would have been able to wander over the roads together, we would have had the sea at our right, the lonely East at our left, and before us, at a great distance, some venturesome inn in which to try our luck at satisfying all those hungers.

At night we would have pressed our faces to the windows, to see families preparing for happiness; and we would have gone down the chimney into rooms that otherwise were too calm, and we would have frightened the people who were about to fall asleep.

In the morning, before dawn, we would have had a swim and we would not have had headaches."
　　　　　— André Gide [122]

_____

———————————————————————————

_____

Index to Quoted Writers

Sources for Quoted Segments

1   Kurt Vonnegut to his daughter, in *Kurt Vonnegut: Letters*, p. 187. Delacorte (2012).
2   This quote, from the 1934 movie "It's a Gift," is probably the source used by Winston Churchill in his famous put-down of Bessie Braddock, who, upon informing Churchill that he was drunk, is said to have been told "Yes, but you are ugly, and in the morning I will be sober."
3   Jane Palen Rushmore, quoted in *Faith and Practice,* p. 2. North Pacific Yearly Meeting, Religious Society of Friends (1986). The original quote reads "our Quaker forefathers," but the sentiment is not limited to one faith, nor indeed to fathers.
4   Karen Armstrong, *Buddha*, p. 109. Penguin (2001).
5   Paul Valéry, "Colloquy Within a Being," *Dialogues* p. 20. Bollingen, Collected Works of Paul Valéry in English, Vol. 4 (1956).
6   Marcus Aurelius, *Meditations*, p. 19. Penguin (2006).
7   Kurt Vonnegut, in a letter to Knox Burger, in *Kurt Vonnegut: Letters*, p. 58. Delacorte (2012).
8   Eric Wilson, *Against Happiness*, p. 55-56. Crichton FSG (2008).
9   Todd Gitlin, "Please Be Disturbed: Triggering Can Be Good for You, Kids." *Tablet*, March 13, 2015.
10 Lisa Jarnot, *Robert Duncan: The Ambassador from Venus, A Biography*, p. 109 (2012).
11 Eric Wilson, *Against Happiness*, p. 19. Crichton FSG (2008).
12 Jacques Berlinerblau, "Hey, Remember Teaching?," in *Chronicle Review*, Jan. 23, 2015, p. B6.
13 Wendell Berry, *What Are People For?*, p. 135. North Point (1990).
14 Ned Rorem, "The Art of the Diary," an interview with J.D. McClatchy in *A Ned Rorem Reader*, p. 12. Yale (2001).
15 John Contreras, *Awakening Your Personal Power*, p. 3. Interactive Media (2009).
16 Bertrand Russell, *In Praise of Idleness*, p. 74. Routledge (2005).
17 C.E.S. Wood, *Too Much Government*, p. 131. Vanguard (1931), *reprinted in* A. Contreras, *Pursuit of Happiness: An Introduction to the Libertarian Ethos of C.E.S. Wood* (2014).

18 Fernando Pessoa, *Selected Prose*, Richard Zenith, ed., p. 237. Grove (2001).

19 Thomas Merton in a letter to Czeslaw Milosz, in *Striving Towards Being: the Letters of Thomas Merton and Czeslaw Milosz*, Robert Faggen, ed., p. 121. Farrar, Straus, Giroux (1997). Younger people may not be familiar with the term "squares." A "square" is a narrow old fuddy-duddy who has probably never tried anything new.

20 Donald Hayes, Cornell University, upon completion of a comparative study of books used in schools. Quoted in William A. Henry III, *In Defense of Elitism*, p. 42. Doubleday (1994).

21 Seneca, *Letters*, No. LXXXVIII p. 151. Penguin (Rev. Ed. 2004).

22 W.H. Auden, *The Prolific and the Devourer*, p. 17. Ecco (1993).

23 Albert Jay Nock, *The Disadvantages of Being Educated and Other Essays*, p. 15. Hallberg (1996).

24 Glenn Jackson, long-time Oregon civic leader, in a speech on education quoted in "Mr. Oregon: Our State's Most Powerful and Least Remembered Leader," John Frohnmayer, *Oregon Quarterly*, Summer 2014 p. 43 (Univ. of Oregon).

25 Robert Grudin, *The Grace of Great Things: Creativity and Innovation*, p. 33. Ticknor and Fields (1990).

26 William A. Henry III, *In Defense of Elitism*, p. 59. Doubleday (1994).

27 John Jay Chapman, in a letter to his wife Elizabeth, Feb. 19, 1910, reprinted in *Unbought Spirit: a John Jay Chapman Reader.* Illinois (1998).

28 Epicurus, fragment, p. 96, *The Essential Epicurus*. Prometheus (1993).

29 José Ortega y Gasset, *The Revolt of the Masses*, p. 49. Norton (1957).

30 Paul Valéry, quote assigned to the ghost of Socrates in "Eupalinos, or The Architect" in *Dialogues* p. 72. Bollingen, Collected Works of Paul Valéry in English, Vol. 4 (1956).

31 John Contreras, *Awakening Your Personal Power*, p. 85. Interactive Media (2009).

32 Paul Valéry, *The Outlook for Intelligence*, p. 140. Princeton, Bollingen series No. 10 (1962).

33 These words are conceived in the mind of Maturin in Patrick O'Brian's novel *The Nutmeg of Consolation*, p. 258. Norton (1991).

34   José Ortega y Gasset, *The Dehumanization of Art*, p. 7. Princeton (1948).

35   C.E.S. Wood, "On Privilege," *Pacific Monthly*, 1911, reprinted in A. Contreras, *Pursuit of Happiness: An Introduction to the Libertarian Ethos of C.E.S. Wood*. (2014).

36   David Miller, *Justice for Earthlings*, p. 113. Cambridge (2013).

37   Angus Kennedy, *Being Cultured: in defense of discrimination*, p. 54. Imprint Academic (2014).

38   Attributed to Aldo Leopold, but possibly a paraphrase of a comment he made about hunting being a solitary endeavor in which doing the right thing is up to the unobserved individual, in *Wildlife in American Culture*, p. 178.

39   Phil Ochs, *Crucifixion* (1966). One of the greatest songs of the late 20th Century, and little known today. Two good covers of this extraordinary song are by Glenn Yarbrough and by Jim & Jean. The original Ochs recording has exceptionally ill-conceived orchestration.

40   John Jay Chapman, *Our Universities*, (1932), reprinted in Alan Contreras, ed., *The Mind on Edge: An Introduction to John Jay Chapman's Philosophy of Higher Education*, p. 104. CraneDance (2013).

41   José Ortega y Gasset, *The Revolt of the Masses*, p. 65. Norton (1957).

42   Robert Grudin, *The Grace of Great Things: Creativity and Innovation*, p. 33. Ticknor and Fields (1990).

43   José Ortega y Gasset, *The Revolt of the Masses*, p. 23. Norton (1957).

44   Seneca, *Letters*, No. XLVIII p. 99-100. Penguin (Rev. Ed. 2004).

45   Paul Valéry, *The Outlook for Intelligence*, p. 203. Princeton, Bollingen series No. 10 (1962).

46   Susan Jacoby, *The Age of American Unreason*, p. 316-317, Pantheon (2008).

47   Matthew Crawford, *The World Beyond Your Head: On Becoming an Individual in an Age of Distraction.* Farrar, Straus, Giroux (2015).

48   James Madison, in the *National Gazette*, Jan. 19, 1792.

49   Albert Camus, *Resistance, Rebellion and Death*, p. 88-89 and 101. Vintage (1995).

50   Paul Valéry to André Gide, in *Self-Portraits: the Gide-Valéry Letters*, Robert Mallet, ed.; June Guicharnaud, trans., p. 305-306. Chicago (1966).

51   Michael Oakeshott, *Rationalism in Politics and Other Essays*, p. 177. Thanks to Matthew Sitman for posting

127

this quote on February 6, 2015, the final day of Andrew Sullivan's incomparable "Daily Dish" blog.

52 David Hume, *An Enquiry Concerning Human Understanding*, p. 109. Barnes & Noble Edition (2004).

53 This widely-circulated quote by Sousa Mendes is reprinted in *The Independent* of October 17, 2010: "Sousa Mendes saved more lives than Schindler so why isn't he a household name too?" by Christian House. For a good book on the work of Sousa Mendes, see José-Alain Fralon, *A Good Man in Evil Times,* Carroll and Graf (2001).

54 Austin Tappan Wright, *Islandia*, p. 861, Rinehart (1942) and subsequent reissuance. Yes, it's a long book, that's why I have only read it seventeen times.

55 I am indebted to my brother John for the notion of "truth vendors," discussed in his book *Gathering Joy* (2007).

56 From the first of a three-part essay on privilege by C.E.S. Wood that originally appeared in *Pacific Monthly* in 1911. Reprinted in A. Contreras, *Pursuit of Happiness: An Introduction to the Libertarian Ethos of Charles Erskine Scott Wood*, p. 107 (2014).

57 Michael P. Lynch, *True To Life*, p. 99, MIT Press (2004).

58 Lucien Price, *Dialogues of Alfred North Whitehead*, p. 138. Little, Brown (1954).

59 Seneca, *Letters*, No. VII p. 43. Penguin (Rev. Ed. 2004).

60 José Ortega y Gasset, *The Revolt of the Masses*, p. 76. Norton (1957).

61 John Contreras, *Gathering Joy*, p. 57. Communication Arts (2007).

62 Dee Hock, former head of VISA, as quoted in Tom Peters and Nancy Austin, *A Passion for Excellence*, p. 250, Collins, London (1985).

63 Jean Findlay describes the transition from lust to love as a "golden conversion" in *Chasing Lost Time: The Life of C. K. Scott Moncrieff,* p. 46. Farrar, Straus & Giroux (2014).

64 Henri Beyle, quoted by Paul Valéry in a letter to André Gide, in *Self-Portraits: the Gide-Valéry Letters*, Robert Mallet, ed.; June Guicharnaud, trans., p. 177. Chicago (1966). Beyle is better known as the novelist Stendhal.

65 Epicurus, Letter to Menoeceus in *The Essential Epicurus* p. 63, Prometheus (1993).

66 Marcus Aurelius, *Meditations*, pp. 12 and 66. Penguin (2006).

67 Albert Jay Nock, quoted in Robert M. Crunden, *The Mind and Art of Albert Jay Nock,* p. 134. Regnery (1964).

Nock stated this premise in slightly different wording in other writings.

68 Seneca, *Letters,* No. LXXVII p. 125. Penguin (Rev. Ed. 2004).

69 C.E.S. Wood, *Too Much Government,* p. 138. Vanguard (1931), reprinted in A. Contreras, *Pursuit of Happiness: An Introduction to the Libertarian Ethos of C.E.S. Wood* (2014). Wood's source for this quote goes back to the father of his friend Billy Craddock.

70 From a speech by Quaker leader Levi Pennington to the Oregon State Bar, September 30, 1927, included in Donald McNichols, *Portrait of a Quaker: Levi T. Pennington,* p. 80. Barclay (1980).

71 George Orwell, "As I Please" 36, *Tribune* of August 4, 1944, reprinted in George Orwell, *Essays,* Everyman's Library (2002).

72 Rebecca Newberger Goldstein, *Plato at the Googleplex: Why Philosophy Won't Go Away,* p. 192. Pantheon (2014)

73 President Obama, in a conversation with 18-year-old Noah McQueen, reported on National Public Radio Feb. 27, 2015.

74 Robert M. Crunden, *The Mind and Art of Albert Jay Nock,* p. 29. Regnery (1964).

75 Albert Camus, *Notebooks 1935-1942,* p. 42. Modern Library (1965).

76 John Stuart Mill, *On Liberty,* p. 122, Barnes & Noble Edition (2004).

77 Yuval Noah Harari, interviewed by Daniel Kahneman in *Edge,* March 5, 2015.

78 Edward Snowden, in an e-mail to Laura Poitras, quoted by Lucy Ferriss in "The Snowden E-mails," *Chronicle Review,* Jan. 16, 2015.

79 Albert Camus, *Notebooks 1935-1942,* p. 59, Modern Library (1965).

80 Florence A. Merriam (Bailey), "Around Our Ranch House," *The Observer* Vol. 7 No 1, Jan. 1896, p. 2; reprinted in *A-birding on a Bronco,* Houghton Mifflin (1896).

81 Marcus Aurelius, *Meditations,* p. 26. Penguin (2006).

82 Bertrand Russell, *In Praise of Idleness,* p. 57. Routledge (2005).

83 Blaise Pascal, *Pensées* (1670).

84 Victor Gollancz, *Our Threatened Values,* p. 34. Gollancz (1946).

85 C.E.S. Wood, *Too Much Government,* p. 219. Vanguard (1931), reprinted in A. Contreras, *Pursuit of Happiness:*

An Introduction to the Libertarian Ethos of C.E.S. Wood (2014).

86 Patrick O'Brian, *The Letter of Marque*, p. 65. Norton (1994). Stephen Maturin states that Saint Teresa made this statement to "my godfather's great-great-grandmother."

87 Albert Camus, *Notebooks 1943-1951*, p. 183. Paragon (1991).

88 Albert Camus, *Notebooks 1943-1951*, p. 249. Paragon (1991).

89 Albert Camus, *Notebooks 1943-1951*, p. 200. Paragon (1991).

90 Francis Bacon, "Of Revenge," *Essays* p. 21. Peter Pauper Press, (undated).

91 This quote is often attributed to English writer and clergyman George Herbert (1593-1633) but may have an earlier origin.

92 Albert Camus, *Notebooks 1935-1942*, p. 5. Modern Library (1965).

93 George Orwell, "What is Science?," *Tribune* of October 26, 1945, reprinted in George Orwell, *Essays*, Everyman's Library (2002).

94 Paul Valéry, *The Outlook for Intelligence*, p. 69. Princeton, Bollingen series No. 10 (1962).

95 Susan Jacoby, *The Age of American Unreason*, p. 23. Pantheon (2008).

96 Rebecca Newberger Goldstein, *Plato at the Googleplex: Why Philosophy Won't Go Away*, p. 392. Pantheon (2014).

97 C.E.S. Wood, "Transmutation of Virtues into Vices," *The Pacific Monthly* 20, no. 4 (October 1908), reprinted in A. Contreras, *Pursuit of Happiness: An Introduction to the Libertarian Ethos of C.E.S. Wood* (2014).

98 Seize the pants!

99 Mary S. Calderone, quoted in *Faith and Practice*, p. 28-29. North Pacific Yearly Meeting, Religious Society of Friends (1986).

100 Laura Kipnis, professor at Northwestern University, in "Sexual Paranoia: How campus rules make students more vulnerable." *Chronicle of Higher Education (Chronicle Review)*, March 6, 2015.

101 Stephen Maturin makes this statement in Patrick O'Brian's novel *Desolation Island*, p. 131. Norton (1994 ed.)

102 Matthew B. Crawford, "The Cost of Paying Attention," *New York Times Sunday Review*, (published online Saturday) March 7, 2015, extracted from the

forthcoming book *The World Beyond Your Head: On Becoming an Individual in an Age of Distraction.*

103 Jean Cocteau, *The Difficulty of Being*, p. 22, Da Capo (1995).

104 Mark C. Taylor, from "The Cult of Speed," *Chronicle of Higher Education*, Oct. 20, 2014 (advance copy for the book *Speed Limits*).

105 Bertrand Russell, *In Praise of Idleness*, p. 135. Routledge (2005).

106 Paul Valéry, *The Outlook for Intelligence*, p. 111. Princeton, Bollingen series No. 10 (1962).

107 Camille Paglia, *Sex, Art and American Culture*, p. 222. Vintage (1992).

108 The early Arab philosopher al-Kindi (805-873) is quoted in Robert Grudin, *Design and Truth*, p. 137. Yale (2010).

109 Montesquieu, quoted in Matthew Arnold, *Culture and Anarchy*, p. 6. MacMillan (1892).

110 Daniel Patrick Moynihan, "The Travail and Fall of Higher Education," in *The Idea of a Modern University* (Sidney Hook, Paul Kurtz and Milo Todorovich, eds., 1974).

111 Alan Contreras, *College and State*, p. 173 (2013).

112 Thomas Merton in a letter to Czeslaw Milosz, in *Striving Towards Being: the Letters of Thomas Merton and Czeslaw Milosz,* Robert Faggen, ed., p. 110. Farrar, Straus, Giroux (1997).

113 Michael Oakeshott, *Virtues of Liberal Learning*, page 102.

114 José Ortega y Gasset, *The Revolt of the Masses*, p. 12. Norton (1957).

115 Paul Valéry, *The Outlook for Intelligence*, p. 85. Princeton, Bollingen series No. 10 (1962).

116 Steve Wasserman, "In Defense of Difficulty," *The American Conservative* (March-April 2015), online March 17, 2015.

117 W. H. Auden, *The Prolific and the Devourer*, p. 7. Ecco (1993).

118 Bertrand Russell, *In Praise of Idleness*, p. 3. Routledge (2005).

119 Robert Grudin, *The Grace of Great Things: Creativity and Innovation*, p. 12. Ticknor and Fields (1990).

120 James Baldwin, *The Cross of Redemption: Uncollected Writings*. Pantheon (2010), p. 74.

121 Albert Camus, *Notebooks 1935-1942*, pp. 85, 92, Modern Library (1965).

122 André Gide to Paul Valéry, in *Self-Portraits: the Gide-Valéry Letters*, Robert Mallet, ed.; June Guicharnaud, trans., p. 151. Chicago (1966).

Notes for a High School Graduate